'Twas the Night Before Jesus

What People are Saying

The story is really good, and the pictures are amazing. This is my new favorite Christmas story.
—**Bentley**, age 11

'Twas the Night Before Jesus is a delightful story that differs from other children's books that tell about the birth of Jesus, because the story doesn't stop at His birth, but also tells about the death and resurrection of Jesus in a way kids can understand. With colorful illustrations, this book should be given as a gift to every child on your Christmas list.
—**Michelle S. Lazurek**, multi-genre author, literary agent, and certified writing coach. Nine-time award-winning author including a two-time Children's Book of the Year award winner. www.michellelazurek.com

A beautiful blend of whimsical illustrations and the portrayal of Jesus's birth, life, death, and resurrection in lilting rhythm and rhyme.
—**Teresa Joyelle Krager**, author. www.tereakrager.com

Children will be drawn to this delightful book into the true reason for Christmas. *'Twas the Night Before Jesus* will capture you with story and illustrations alike. A beautiful telling of the birth of Christ.
—**Michele McCarthy**, award-winning author for *Aunt Ida Clare*. 2021 Best Fiction Children's Book, 1st Place Golden Scrolls, and 2021 Children's Fiction Book of the Year/Christian Market Book Award. www.michelemccarthybooks.com

'Twas the Night Before Jesus

Donna Wyland
Illustrated by Courtney Smith

ELK LAKE PUBLISHING INC

PUBLISHING THE POSITIVE
Plymouth, Massachusetts

Cover and Interior Design: Courtney Smith, Derinda Babcock

Editor(s): Derinda Babcock, Deb Haggerty

Illustrations: Courtney Smith

PUBLISHED BY: Elk Lake Publishing, Inc., 35 Dogwood Drive, Plymouth, MA 02360, 2021

_____

Library Cataloging Data

Names: Wyland, Donna (Donna Wyland)

'Twas the Night Before Jesus / Donna Wyland

42 p. 21.6 cm × 21.6 cm (8. 5 in × 8. 5 in.)

Identifiers: ISBN-13: 978-1-64949-388-0 (paperback) | 978-1-64949-389-7 (trade paperback) | 978-1-64949-390-3 (trade hardcover) | 978-1-64949-391-0 (ebook)

Key Words: Life of Christ; True meaning of Christmas; Angels; Shepherds; King Herod; Salvation plan; Resurrection of Jesus

Library of Congress Control Number: 2021946462 Nonfiction

Author's Dedication

To my parents, John and Janet Schroeder, who instilled in me a love for God and for Christmas.

’Twas the night before Jesus
and all through the land,
Lived people not knowing
that God would be man.

The shepherds were resting,
their flocks lying near,
Unaware that the Christ-child
soon would appear.

When Joseph was told
there was no place to stay,
An innkeeper offered
his stable and hay.

4

The small stall was filled
with the innkeeper's sheep,
With cattle and chickens
too noisy to sleep.

The Virgin was weary,
yet, how could she rest?
The Savior was coming,
the Lord manifest!

In humble surroundings
Christ Jesus was born.
Wrapped in cloth the babe lay
in a trough, rough and worn.

8

Shepherds looked up
and saw angels just then
Singing, "Glory to God,
and on earth peace to men."

Then God hung a star
in the sky that shone bright
And summoned three Wise Men
to follow its light.

The Magi rode camels
for miles to the place
Where Jesus was staying,
his home lit with grace.

They bowed low and worshiped
the child in their way,
Then offered him treasures
with little delay.

14

King Herod had asked them
to find the young child
So he could, himself,
worship Jesus a while.

But God, in a dream,
told the Magi to go
A different way home,
a new way he would show.

The child was in danger
Joseph saw in a dream.
So, to Egypt they fled
to avoid Herod's scheme.

When the wicked king died,
young Joseph was told
To move once again,
and let God's plan unfold.

They walked for ten days
with the sand whirling 'round;
Through the desert and hills
till the right place was found.

They settled in Nazareth
till Christ was a man.
John the Baptist announced
God's salvation plan.

"Repent!" John proclaimed.
"The kingdom is near."
When he baptized Christ Jesus,
God's will became clear.

A dove slowly landed
beside Jesus's head.
"This is My Son,"
from heaven, God said.

22

Jesus preached, and he healed.
he taught, and he fed.
Then he ate his last meal,
slept upon his last bed.

Jesus died on a cross,
then for three days he lay
In a tomb, in a cave,
until the third day.

While Mary stood weeping
two angels in white
Spoke softly to her,
filled the dark tomb with light.

24

She turned and saw Jesus,
though wasn't he dead?
When he spoke, she cried, "Teacher!"
He arose as he'd said!

He saw his disciples
first, Peter and John,
Then twelve in a locked room,
Alive! He had won!

Five hundred then saw him
and instantly knew.
His Father was faithful.
God's promise was true.

Jesus died for our sins
to save us from death.
He fills us with peace,
with his Spirit, his breath.

28

Today we are blessed
with the gift of his love.
He sits at the Father's
right hand up above.

29

He's waiting to greet us.
one day we will see,
Our heavenly home
filled with God's family.

Until then, on Christmas,
we say with delight,
" 'Happy Birthday to Jesus!'
and to all a good night."

About the Author

DONNA WYLAND is an award-winning author, editor, and coach who believes in writing books that entertain, encourage, and inspire. Her bestselling children's book, *Your Home in Heaven*, sold thousands of copies and was gifted to more than 4,000 children around the world through churches, schools, and various ministry organizations in the US and abroad.

Reprinted in 2020 by Elk Lake Publishing, Inc., *Your Home in Heaven* has become a classic story that shares the love of God and the hope of heaven with an increasing number of children. *If I Could Ask Jesus*, Donna's premier Christian bedtime story is bringing young hearts closer to God too.

Donna lives in Ohio with her husband and a couple of bunnies that hide under the bushes outside. She loves to read, ski, jump on the trampoline with her grandson, and cross items off of her personal Bucket List. To connect, email donna@donnawyland.com.

About the Illustrator

COURTNEY SMITH grew up in southwestern Colorado, and later attended college at Regis University, where she met and married a handsome rocket scientist. Together, they have welcomed five children and live in Franktown, Colorado. Courtney raises Great Pyrenees puppies, teaches CPR, travels internationally with USA Olympic wrestling hopefuls as an athletic trainer, and cheers on her children. In her free time, she loves to draw and sketch, creating images to enhance incredible stories.

CPSIA information can be obtained
at www.ICGtesting.com
Printed in the USA
BVHW091438141221
624006BV00008B/783